Contents

Abstract

This book will explore the development of standard form contracts, focusing on their salience in the digital age. It will consider arguments surrounding the idea that clicking "I agree" is analogous to a signature on a paper contract. This book aims to explore the history of boilerplates and how they're applied in contemporary UK. This will uncover how boilerplates in contracts between businesses and consumers.

Second, this book will critically analyse the current legal controls that oversee standard form contracting. It will be argued that in light of the developments to the electronic environment, the present legal controls are unsatisfactory in protecting consumer contractual rights. This book proposes the establishment of an independent authority, namely the "Standard Form Consumer Contracts Authority". This independent body will be accountable to Parliament and will possess legislative powers to regulate firms which adopt standard form contracts, both in the paper and virtual arena.

Introduction

Standard form contracts have been subject to much criticism within the realms of legal academia. Standard form contracts have been given various descriptions, such as "contracts of adhesion" and "standardised contracts", which all semantically refer to the same construct. A standard form contract is a contract in which the terms and conditions are one-sided, putting the other party in an non-negotiable position; with boilerplates being the specific, reproduced terms.

Its substance and form are typically devised by a large firm[1], stipulating terms which are beneficial to the firm specifically. It is then used in every

---

[1] Small firms often devise boilerplate agreements too.

bargain dealing with the same product or service[2]. It has been argued that the insurgence of large scale enterprise with its mass production and mass distribution has saw the inevitable development of a new contract – the standardised mass contract[3].

Friedrich Kessler provided clarity as to what standard form is and highlighted some key attributes: typically used by businesses with a "strong bargaining power"; drafter had a monopolistic position or used the same contract as competitors (contractual freeriding); weaker party understood the legal consequences of the

---

[2] Fredrich Kessler, 'Contracts of Adhesion – Some Thoughts About Freedom Of Contract' [1943] Columbia Law Review 629.

[3] Otto Prausnitz, 'The Standardisation of Commercial Contracts in English and Continental Law' [1937] Harvard Law Review 700.

contract in a "vague manner"; and terms presented in a "take it or leave it" manner"[4]. This type of contract has revolutionised the way in which businesses contract with consumers, and with technological developments, it has become increasingly prevalent on the internet. In assessing the balance of bargaining power between businesses and consumers, we can see that it tips greatly in favour of the former.

The aim of this book is to explore the nature of standard form contracts, considering arguments in support of their existence, as well as the opposing arguments. In understanding the basic ideas of standard form, we will then look to the

---

[4] Fredrich Kessler, 'Contracts of Adhesion – Some Thoughts About Freedom Of Contract' [1943] Columbia Law Review 629

unique nature of contracts formulated online and how it has altered the bargaining dynamic.

First, we will look to the reasons as to why standard form contracts have become a revolutionary necessity in the world of contracting. Second, justifications for standard form contracts will be considered and how these justifications apply to e-commerce. It will then consider the implications that consumers face on a daily basis. Once the implications have been assessed, current legislative measures will be analysed, placing their efficacy under a normative lens.

In concluding this book, possible legislative and market reforms will be discussed. It is my suggestion that standard for contracts have altered the dynamic in which businesses and consumers contract, undermining and contradicting the neo-classical theory of free bargaining. Although this does not come without its benefits, the shift to electronic contracting has shaped it in such a way that warrants intervention. As it will be argued, consumers are likely to be unmindful when purporting to these agreements; not being entirely sure as to what they have agreed to. It is my argument that the digital age has allowed for contract in which assent is driven by materialism rather than by an understanding of one's position.

Consumers are less concerned about the terms that they agree to and are driven by factors such as best quality and best price. As such, it should be the responsibility of an independent authority to oversee standard form contracting between businesses and consumers. Once conventional reforms have been assessed, I will argue that consumers will respond better to reforms that highlight the terms which are favourable to the consumer, or readily draws unfavourable terms to their attention.

One way this can be achieved is by providing a forum in which competitor contracts can be assessed by rating, such as a "compare the contract" website. This website could compare contracts by industry and give a detailed analysis of important standardised terms which have been adopted by particular firms in that industry. A consume could look for mobile phone contracts offered by particular service providers, and then compare these contracts to see which firms adopt certain operational terms, such as arbitration clauses, or choice of forum clauses. Typically, comparison websites focus on comparing prices, but there is scope for comparing contracts by other terms.

Objective Theory of Contract

Historically, contracts required a "meeting of minds" to be legally recognised[5]. However in contemporary contracting, it has been acknowledged that no actual subjectivity is required. It has been argued that this is due to the introspectivity of man; the mind of a human being unknown and uncertain[6]. In accordance with this recognition, the courts have shifted towards an "objective" reality[7]. The courts introduced a test of "reasonableness" and focused on how words and actions would be

---

[5] Michael Meyerson, 'The Reunification of Contract Law: The Objective Theory of Consumer Form Contracts' [1993] Miami Law Review 1263, citing Edward Allan Farnsworth, 'Meaning in the Law of Contracts' [1967] Yale Law Journal 943.

[6] Ibid.

[7] Ibid.

understood by the reasonable man. In *Smith v Hughes*, Blackburn J famously opined:

"If, whatever a man's real intention may be, he so conducts himself that a reasonable man would believe that he was assenting to the terms proposed by the other party, and that the other party upon that believe enters into the contract with him, the man thus conducting himself would be equally bound as if he had intended to agree to the other party's terms"[8].

This case highlights the importance of certainty in contractual agreements. This importance has been consistently acknowledged throughout

---

[8] [1871] LR 6 QB 597, QBD (Blackburn J).

judicial developments. As such, the courts have created a duty to read; in the passive sense that a person is bound by a contract that they have signed – irrespective of whether they have read the terms. This was established in *L'Estrange v Graucob*[9]. This case still resonates importance as a basic tenet to the incorporation of terms into a contract. It must be noted that this rule is not absolute and comes with various qualifications (which will be discussed later in the evaluation of legislation).

As previously discussed, it is widely accepted that consumers do not read the contracts that they assent to. However, it is right to assume that

---

[9] [1934] 2 KB 394.

they know core terms such as price and quantity. In the electronic environment, consumers still do not read the terms of the contract they assent to. It could be argued that they are less likely to read the terms online than they would on paper. It has been contended that the common law of contracts has strived for the path of logical progression[10]. Further, it has been contended that this took a wrong turn when the logical assumption that a merchant's signature implied assent to negotiated terms, was mistakenly applied to consumer form contracts[11].

It is often difficult to discern the objective meaning of a consumer's signature and thus an issue of objectivity is raised when it is well known

---

[10] Michael Meyerson, 'The Reunification of Contract Law: The Objective Theory of Consumer Form Contracts' [1993] Miami Law Review 1263.

[11] Ibid at p.1271.

that consumers do not read the contracts that they sign. It has been argued that merchants and sellers who know that consumers do not read the terms have no objective basis for claiming that the consumers agreed to those terms[12]. The law has given drafters of form contracts the power to impose their will on suspecting and vulnerable individuals[13]. When agreeing to electronic contracts, there is a degree of uncertainty as to whether clicking "I agree" is equivalent to a signature for the purposes of the incorporation of standard terms. Macdonald argues this in the negative and contents that a click should not be paid with the same regard as agreeing to a contract by signature, for the purposes of the

---

[12] Ibid.

[13] Ibid at p.1272.

L'Estrange[14] case. She notes "...when the law is applied in a new context the change in significance of a particular aspect may need to be recognised"[15].

Although I am sympathetic to her concern, I am not convinced that this should be reflected in the law. The significance of the *L'Estrange* decision is that a signature evidences incorporation of terms into the contract. It must be noted that a signature is but one way in which the relying party can incorporate terms into a contract. I understand Macdonald's position as the electronic arena does create cause for concern, especially with the vagueness of the "I agree" button.

---

[14] Elizabeth Macdonald, 'Incorporation of Terms in Website Contracting – clicking "I agree'" [2011] Journal of Contract Law 198.

[15] Ibid at p.12.

Depending on how the label is constructed, the question as to what the consumer has agreed to still remains. This could easily be remedied if the law provided harmonisation to "I agree" caveats. It would be hard for one to rebut presence of an actual agreement if the button said "I have read and agree to the website owner's presented terms".

Macdonald's argument is unconvincing because it makes commercial sense to analogise a signature to a click. The digital age was the next evolutionary step for the contract arena. I contend that a signature should be translated into the electronic arena by a click, on the proviso that the click button is absent of any ambiguities and what is being agreed to is easily discernible. To suggest otherwise would be commercially detrimental, and even though some contend that the click is a tenuous sign of agreement, it is better to have some form of acknowledgement than none at all. I contend that the law should build upon this acknowledgment and give it a great deal of oversight.

Paper and Virtual Boilerplate: A Comparison

Standard form contracts have been used for over two centuries, with their first use being for marine insurance in the 19th Century[16]. Standard form contracts have been synonymously described as "contracts of adhesion", and first entered into American jurisprudence by the work of Edwin Patterson, as he described the nature of an insurance contract as something being "adhered" to.; because the insured had "little choice over the terms"[17]. It was the insurance industry's reliance on form contracts which

---

[16] Michael Meyerson, 'The Reunification of Contract Law: The Objective Theory of Consumer Form Contracts' [1993] Miami Law Review 1263

[17] Edwin Patterson, 'The Delivery of a Life-Insurance Policy' [1919] Harvard Law Review 198.

marked a radical departure from the traditional negotiated contract[18]. Prausnitz strikingly argued:

"No longer do individuals bargain for this or that provision in the contract... the control of the wording of those contracts has passed into the hands of the concern, and the drafting into the hands of its legal advisor... In the trades affected it is henceforth futile for an individual to attempt any modification, and incorrect for the economist and lawyer to classify or judge such arrangements as standing on an equal footing with individual agreements"[19].

---

[18] Michael Meyerson, 'The Reunification of Contract Law: The Objective Theory of Consumer Form Contracts' [1993] Miami Law Review 1263

[19] Otto Prausnitz, 'The Standardisation of Commercial Contracts in English and Continental Law' [1937], cited by Michael Meyerson, 'The Reunification of Contract Law: The Objective Theory of Consumer Form Contracts' [1993] Miami Law Review 1263.

This highlights the impact placed on traditional contractual negotiations by the increasingly used form contract. It also opens doors to wider contemporary debate concerning the problems associated with form contracts; particularly between businesses and consumers. As will be seen throughout this book, there is a significant dichotomy within the dialogue surrounding this debate. This division exists between academics who see form contracts as equally valid to negotiated, individual contracts, and the other half who do not. It is the latter form of opinion which is central to the discussion in this paper, as it uncovers greater problems associated with form contracts. It is important to uncover these underlying problems as it will give a clearer picture as to the relationship between businesses and consumers; giving us a better understanding of the imbalance of power that exists between the parties. This in turn gives stronger justification for reform. This group of commentators recognise that consumer form contracts create special risks and problems[20]. This book looks into these risks and problems in detail and how they translate into the online arena.

As businesses have moved to the internet to conduct their dealings, it has become commonplace for consumers to contract by "clicking to agree" on websites[21] and installing

---

[20] Ibid at p. 1264.

[21] David Slawson, 'Standard Form Contracts and Democratic Control of Lawmaking Power' [1971] Harvard Law Review 529.

computer programs. "Browsewrap" and "clickwrap" are two of the main ways in which consumers enter into contracts digitally. Browsewrap contracts refer to those in which websites will provide some tenuous hyperlink to a set of terms and conditions.

Businesses often refer to it as their "Terms of Service" (TOS) or "Conditions of Use" (COU). Even just visiting the website constitutes an acceptance of the terms[22]. Shrinkwrap contracts predominantly involve software licenses which are agreed to after the consumer opens the product[23]. The term "shrinkwrap" has been coined with reference to the fact that consumers find

---

[22] Robert A. Hillman and Jeffrey J. Rachlinski, 'Standard Form Contracting in the Electronic Age' [2002] New York University Law Review 77(2)

[23] Ibid at p.37

themselves typically bound to the license once they open the shrinkwrapped packaging of the product. Hillman and Rachlinski have argued "the widespread availability of information technologies and the Internet in particular, has significantly changed consumer activity"[24]. Therefore it can be argued that this shift in consumer activity has been responded to proactively by businesses. This begs the question: has the internet changed the dynamic of standard form contracting? Hillman and Rachlinski seem to argue not, or they suggest that it hasn't changed it to the point of calling for a different legal regime[25]. Although their argument is in stark contrast to the theme of this

---

[24] Ibid at p.36.

[25] Ibid at p.5.

book, I do agree with them in that there is a particular symmetry between paper and electronic standard form contracts; although the symmetry I believe to be pertinent are the implications for the consumer. It is therefore vital to look at the issues that paper and electronic form contracts have in common, and look at the extent to which the electronic environment has affected the contract arena.

As previously discussed, the nature of standard form systematically serves the interests of businesses, as it is the business that spends a considerable amount of time devising the contract. Hillman and Rachlinski acknowledge the fact that "businesses in both the paper and electronic contexts have incentives and abilities to induce consumers to accept standard terms that are not in the consumers' best interest"[26]. One commonality to exist is that there is an experienced business which drafts the standard terms, and inexperienced consumers that give assent to it. This assent is further complicated by the unmindful position that consumers place themselves in. In short, consumers simply do not read the standard form contracts that they agree to. Even if consumers did read the terms, it is very unlikely that they would understand the content. It has been argued that the courts have struggled to balance the importance of enforcing reasonable terms against the need to defend consumers from exploitation[27]. The central issue

---

[26] Ibid.

[27] Todd Rakoff, 'Contracts of Adhesion, An Essay in Reconstruction' [1983] Harvard Law Review 1173.

surrounding boilerplates is the degree of judicial oversight that should be afforded to them. This central issue has been underpinned by the unfortunate reality that consumers do not read the terms.

One key difference is that with paper contracts, there is usually personal engagement between the consumer and the agent of the business. Whether it is buying a mobile phone contract or a cinema ticket, the agent presents to the customer a copy of standard terms. The consumer is more likely to be aware of the one-sidedness of a standard form contract. Consumers are aware that the terms presented to them are non-negotiable. They base this awareness on the fact that either the agent is not disposed to bargain over the boilerplates, or lacks the authority to do so[28]. It is often the case that consumers feel pressured to sign the contract quickly, to avoid the feeling of awkwardness[29]. Consumers may feel as though they are being confrontational towards the agent, showing a degree of distrust[30]. Furthermore, the consumer does not want to spend more time on the contract than they have to. This is all evidence of the social pressures that consumers face in the paper arena; to sign contracts quickly without informing themselves of the terms.

---

[28] Melvin Eisenberg, 'The Limits of Cognition and the Limits of Contract' [1995] Stanford Law Review 221.

[29] Ibid at p.243

[30] Ibid.

By contrast, in the virtual arena, consumers cannot negotiate terms because there is no live agent to facilitate the negotiation. One further problem contributed by the virtual arena is that the absence of a live agent means the consumer cannot find answers to their possible questions. This is a "take-it-or-leave-it" contract in its purest form[31]. Although this may be one-sided, it has been argued that boilerplate is essential to e-commerce as negotiating terms electronically could be problematic. Negotiation would require the electronic transaction to be interrupted and using a human agent to conduct the negotiations[32]. The lack of human agents is

---

[31] Take it or leave it in the sense that the absence of negotiation means the consumer will have to go elsewhere if they aren't happy with the terms.

[32] Richard Gomulkiewicz, 'The License is the Product: Comments on the Promise of Article 2B for Software and Information Licensing' [1998] Berkeley Technology Law Journal 897.

critical to the efficiency that electronic contracts so enjoy[33].

This links to the new dynamic that electronic contracting has brought to the agreement arena. As previously discussed, there is great importance placed upon a signature in a contract. The courts have consistently denoted a signature to signal consent and thus creating a binding agreement. Consumers have also grown accustomed to this importance and know the implications that follow "signing on the dotted line". With relation to clicking "I agree", it is questionable whether consumers hold this to the same level of regard.

---

[33] Ibid at p.897.

Social factors and pressures from the paper world cannot be translated into its virtual counterpart, due to the lack of live social interaction. There will be the lack of confrontational feeling on behalf of the consumer. It has been argued that in lack of pressures to sign, the consumer finds himself with more time to read the terms and thus become more knowledgeable about their position[34]. I find this argument to be unconvincing. Being given an opportunity to read and actually doing it are to distinct things. Although this is not absolute, it has been noted that the relative target market of e-commerce is the younger generation[35]. Rather than consumers seeing internet contracting as an opportunity to

---

[34] Robert A. Hillman and Jeffrey J. Rachlinski, 'Standard Form Contracting in the Electronic Age'. [2002] New York University Law Review 77(2)

[35] Ibid at p.41.

take their time to understand their position, they have seen efficacy and speed. Consumers have become "click happy" when it comes to electronic transactions and have used e-commerce as a way of saving time[36]. Psychologists have argued that an exploration of the internet induces a sense of impatience and frustration on part of the user[37]. This is potentially dangerous when it comes to formulating agreements. Thus we can see that internet contracting has provided a forum which exacerbates the eagerness of the consumer to agree to the terms given, rather than utilising the opportunity given in absence of paper-associated social pressures. Consumes underestimate the power of a "click".

---

[36] Ibid.

[37] Patricia Wallace, *The Psychology of the Internet* (1st edn, Cambridge University Press 2001), ch.6.

In the absence of social pressures, businesses have used the internet as a tool in order to manipulate consumers into rushing consent. The convoluted nature of the terms is something that is present both in the paper and virtual arena. As previously argued, contracts are devised by the business itself. It will be imbibed with complex legal jargon that would be difficult even learned in the law to understand[38]. There is greater scope for manipulation in the virtual arena as there are avenues which the business can take to change the way the terms are perceived and presented.

Certain methods of presentation can affect the propensity of consumers to read terms. This was

---

[38] Ibid at p.49

exemplified in the US case *Williams v America Online Inc*[39] in which the plaintiffs were subscribers to AOL. As subscribers, the plaintiffs were required to install "AOL Version 5.0" as per the terms of subscription. Upon installation, the plaintiffs alleged their computers to have been damaged by software distributed by AOL. Specifically, the installation of AOL Version 5.0 caused unauthorised changes to the configuration of their computers and so could no longer access non-AOL Internet Service Providers. The plaintiffs also alleged that they were no longer able to run non-AOL email programs and were unable to access personal information and files.

---

[39] 2001 WL 135825

This harm occurred prior to agreeing to AOL's standard "Terms of Service". The court gave judgment to the plaintiffs and found that in order to access the TOS, the plaintiffs had to specifically request it twice by overriding the default settings. This case is important in illustrating how businesses can conceal their terms by manipulating their presentation. This also shows how businesses can and do take advantage of consumer unmindfulness.

Justifying Boilerplate

This book looks in considerable detail at the implications and issues that arise when concerned with standard form contracts, and how that has translated into the digital arena. Despite boilerplate contracts affording many problems, they are becoming increasingly popular and come without prohibition.

Thus it is important to look at why this is the case and the arguments justifying them. IN attempting to balance the argument, it can be said that there are economic benefits in support of standard form contracts. From an economic standpoint, it has been argued that experienced businesses best understand their risks and can therefore determine what they can bear. By doing this, they can also determine what risks should be allocated to the consumer[40]. Economic principles dictate that careful allocation of these risks minimises the cost of whatever the business is offering (goods or services)[41]. Although this seems efficient and provides consumers with the immediate benefit of a reduced price, it also uncovers issues with uniformity. The primary benefit of allocating risk is to the business. The best allocation of risks is not likely to vary between businesses within a particular industry. This lack of variation is demonstrated by homogeneity in standard terms; businesses will offer terms that are similar to their competitors[42].

---

[40] Fredrich Kessler, 'Contracts of Adhesion – Some Thoughts About Freedom Of Contract' [1943] Columbia Law Review 629.

[41] Ibid at p.632

[42] Ibid.

With this type of free-riding, standard terms also save costs spent on litigation due to withstanding judicial scrutiny[43]. Businesses will incorporate not only standard terms that effectively allocate risks, but ones that have also stood up in court. This type of certainty is appealing to businesses because they can predict outcomes if a dispute were to arise.

Meyerson, however, rightfully points out that the process which allows businesses to identify the efficient allocation of risks comes with an opportunity to exploit consumers[44]. In the lack of appreciation that consumers have for their

---

[43] Marcel Khan and Michael Klausner, 'Path Dependence in Corporate Contracting: Increasing Returns, Herd Behaviour, and Cognitive Biases' [1996] Washington University Law Quarterly 347.

[44] Michael Meyerson, 'The Reunification of Contract Law: The Objective Theory of Consumer Form Contracts' [1993] Miami Law Review 1263

contractual position, businesses have an

opportunity to impose hidden risks on

consumers[45].

Radin has noted that repeated use of standard

terms offers consumers a better chance of

understanding the meaning of the terms and

gives the courts opportunity to sift out the

onerous ones "... fostering the evolution of terms

migrating towards the reasonable"[46]. Although I

agree with her in that it provides the court with

an opportunity to invalidate the onerous terms, I

am sceptical as to the likelihood that consumers

will develop an understanding of the terms. The

---

[45] Robert A. Hillman and Jeffrey J. Rachlinski, 'Standard Form Contracting in the Electronic Age' [2002] New York University Law Review 77(2), p12.

[46] Margaret J. Radin, 'Humans, Computers and Binding Commitment' [2000] Indiana Law Journal 1125, p.1347

chance to understand, and actually understanding are two different ideas; which rests on the false assumption that consumers will read the terms in the first place.

In assessing justifications of standard form, there is a body of literature which supports the idea that boilerplates are justified because they are freely consented to by its recipients. In the absence of consumers not reading the terms, "consent", and "agreement" have been contested as to their definition and relationship. With the emergence of standard form, we can see that their definitions have evolved and the notion of "assent" has become increasingly important. For Radin, the use of the word "agreement" was the traditional word to use in contracts but does not necessarily make it an agreement by merely using the label "agreement". She further argues that the use of such a word when it comes to boilerplate has seen a "devolution or decay of the concept of voluntariness"[47]. The use of the word "agreement" has been reduced to "consent" and in the light of consumers not reading the terms, this has been further reduced to "assent"[48]. In distinction, Radin contends that "agreement" implies a two-way process, with two parties coming to an agreement whereas "consent" seems to be one-sided, with a proposition by one party and acceptance by the other[49]. The issue of consent in standard form contracts highlight the

---

[47] Ibid.

[48] Ibid.

[49] Ibid at p.83.

contradiction that it brings in relation to the neo-classical contract argument. In light of this, Barnett raises the important question:

"If contract is based on promise, then how can someone have promised to do something in a writing he or she has not and was not expected to have read?"[50].

In "assenting" to electronic boilerplate, it seems that there is no distinction in terms of method; signing on the dotted line and clicking "I agree" have the legal significance. Thus, if there is a distinction, it will be artificial. Although it is justifiable for a firm to hold clicking "I agree" as

---

[50] Randy Barnett, 'Consenting to Form Contracts' [2002] Fordham Law Review 627 p.628.

an assent to the terms, I submit that there is a greater underestimation of risk on part of the consumer in doing this. Consumers who click "I agree" are unlikely to have at the forefront of their mind an understanding of the terms behind the transaction, or even an understanding of their existence. Those who click will not be intending to consent to the terms which work to deprive the consumer of their rights[51].

As a result, commentators have cast a different light on "consent" to boilerplates. Karl Llewellyn most notably contributes to this discourse with his idea of "blanket assent" to contracts[52]. Llewellyn argues that rather than focusing on an

---

[51] Margaret J. Radin, 'Boilerplate: The Fine Print, Vanishing Rights, and The Rule of Law' (Princeton University Press, 2013) p.88

[52] Karl Llewellyn, *The Common Law Tradition: Deciding Appeals* (1960) p.370

"assent" to boilerplate clauses, it is better to argued that what has happened is a blanket assent to the broad transaction[53]. He defends his position as he contends that when regarding the specifics in a standard form contract, there is no assent at all. He argues:

"What has in fact been assented to, specifically, are the few dickered terms, and the more broad type of the transaction... the fine print which has not been read has no business to cut under the reasonable meaning of those dickered terms which constitute the dominant and only real expression of agreement, but much of it commonly belongs in"[54].

---

[53] Ibid.
[54] Ibid.

In consideration of this "blanket assent", it has been argued that contract law is settling for something less than real consent. Brian Bix argues:

"...consent in the robust sense expressed by the ideal of 'freedom of contract' is absent in the vast majority of the contracts we enter into these days, but its absence does little to affect the enforceability of these contracts"[55].

This accurately encapsulates the reality of a standard form transaction. Although Bix encapsulates this shortfall, he argues for its existence based on economic efficiency grounds.

---

[55] Brian Bix, *Contracts, in the Ethics of Consent* (Franklin G. Miller and Alan Wertheimer, eds 2010) p.251.

He argues that making too many commercial transactions subject to challenge on consent/voluntariness grounds would undermine the predictability of enforcement, which is needed for vibrant economic activity[56].

In justifying boilerplate, we have seen the economic benefits which it provides. Boilerplate terms do provide some efficiencies and economic prosperity arguably depends on them. It seems impossible to think of a stability in a mass-market system which operates without standardised contracts. It is an obvious submission that negotiating contractual terms would take time and thus stagnating economic

---

[56] Ibid.

activity. However, in supporting this fast-paced market with standardisation, the law has accepted a structure which is something less than a real consent to the terms. In its digital translation, we can see that this decay has been furthered. Llewellyns "blanket assent" theory plays a more relevant part to e-commerce as consumers have grown to clicking "I agree" in an idiosyncratic fashion. In the online arena, the consumer's ignorance has more continuity in comparison to its paper counterpart. In shrinkwrap agreements, software is often improved and uses the internet in order to be able to download updates. For example, Microsoft Office releases updates frequently and thus requires new downloads each time[57]. In this continuity, it has become easier for businesses to modify its terms. The updated terms are presented in the same fashion as the original agreement; consumers still remain unaware. Therefore consumers are unaware of terms in the first instance and continue to be so throughout the changing of the terms. This creates cause for concern because in the "click happy" habit of consumers, they will be continuously assenting to new terms whilst remaining unmindful of the substantive change. At best, the consumer will know that there has been a change to the terms (this usually presents itself in the form of "I

---

[57] See http://windows.microsoft.com/en-gb/windows/update-microsoft-office#1TC=windows-7.

agree to the change in terms"), but the consumer will not know for certain what has changed.

I do not contend that boilerplates should be rendered legally invalid; I call for greater judicial oversight in light of the cause for concern mentioned above. Standardisation of contract terms has resulted in what Radin refers to as a decay of voluntariness. In accepting boilerplate, consent has been degraded to blanket coverage of the entire contract; including terms unseen. Llewellyn's blanket assent argument presents dangers to the digital environment as contracts formed within it have the potential to be in a constant change of flux. The unilateral variation of the contract comes with the same level of ignorance that the initial agreement came with.

In the exploitative behaviour of businesses, it is not impossible to think of a contract varied so much to the extent that it no longer reflects the initial agreement; discoverable only in the event of a dispute.

Reconceptualising Consent: As-Product

So far this book has explored the role of consent

in contractual agreements, and how boilerplate

has degraded it to a "blanket assent". Radin

contends that contract-as-consent is the

traditional model which underpins our

understanding of contractual commitment[58]. It

involves a meeting of minds or at least a consent.

Radin conceptualises consent as "...a knowing

understanding of what one is doing in a context

in which it actually possible for one to do

otherwise, and an affirmative action in doing

something, rather than a merely passive

acquiescence in accepting something"[59].

---

[58] Margaret J. Radin, 'Humans, Computers and Binding Commitment' [2000] Indiana Law Journal 1125, p.1124.

[59] Ibid at p.1125.

As Barnett argues, a person signing a standard form contract does not subjectively and consciously assent to the terms that go unread[60]. He also rightly contends that someone offering such terms cannot have reasonably thought that the other party subjectively consented and thus there is no objective agreement[61]. This accurately reflects the realities of boilerplate contracts going largely unread, in both discussed realms. It also demonstrates how firms are aware of consumers being unmindful when purporting to such agreements. Rakoff argues that the terms which are in the parties' interest to focus on are labelled "visible terms"[62], this relates to the price,

---

[60] Randy Barnett, 'Consenting to Form Contracts' [2002] Fordham Law Review 627 p.632.

[61] Ibid.

[62] Todd Rakoff, 'Contracts of Adhesion, An Essay in Reconstruction' [1983] Harvard Law Review 1173, p.1251.

description, and quantity of the product. The terms which consumers do not tend to focus on are what Rakoff describes as "invisible"[63]. Although some commentators have been cautious of Rakoff's argument regarding unread terms being "invisible" (as this is not to be taken literally), I agree with him in that there is a distinction between what terms consumers do and do not concern themselves with; ironically the terms unconcerned are those which have the most adverse effect upon consumer rights.

It seems rational to be concerned with terms relating to the essence of the agreement, but this also does not come at the expense of not being

---

[63] Ibid.

mindful of what rights may have been affected or waivered. Llewellyn disregarded this term distinction and held that consumers give a blanket assent, to the terms which have been seen and to the terms which have not[64]. It could be argued that clicking "I agree" is manifest to agreeing to the entirety of a TOS; agreeing to the unread obligations.

As a result of this degradation of consent, commentators have reconceptualised consent and its relationship to the contract. Economics call this model "contract-as-product", and renders terms as part of the product and not being a separable bargain[65]. In relation to unread terms

---

[64] Karl Llewellyn *The Common Law Tradition: Deciding Appeals* (1960) p.370.
[65] Ibid.

Radin argues that they are no more and no less significant than unseen internal design features[66]. This is an interesting way of reconceptualising standard form contracts in wake of consumers not reading them. I contend that this model is more applicable to the online boilerplate as the nature of digitisation allows for an intangible product, whilst still applying to tangible goods. I am sceptical as to applying the contract-as-product model to the paper world and to tangible products; treating terms as integral to the product is an artificial conflation. It seems illogical to hold terms as part and parcel of certain tangible products, such as the purchase of food. In the virtual arena, it is easier to treat

---

[66] Margaret J. Radin, 'Humans, Computers and Binding Commitment' [2000] Indiana Law Journal 1125.

terms as part of the product in shrinkwrap contracts and the purchase of software. Contract-as-product is easier to apply to electronic agreements also because of the state of constant change that these agreements find themselves in. As previously argued, digitised agreements and uses of software undergo continuous change. When software companies provide updates to the product, variation and updates to terms come in conjunction.

Therefore, the contract-as-product model offers a new way of thinking about consent and how it links to the contract. Standard form contracting has become problematic in the requirement of consent. It has become problematic as it is increasingly difficult to maintain the minimum standard if consent as described by Radin. The online arena has only exacerbated this issue further, allowing for contracts to exist which have unlimited scope for continuous development. Rather than attempting to reform the contract, an attempt at reforming the standard of consent has come about instead. The contract-as-product model alters the traditional relationship between the contract and the consent to it. It is now thought that the terms are integral to the product, rather than the driving force to it. The issue of unread terms is ameliorated in that it has become an unseen part of the product. Although this is an interesting reconceptualisation, one must be cautious of its application in every agreement. I have already raised issues of artificial conflation and that contract-as-product is a model best kept for the digital arena; for contracts that have the potential to be updated frequently. If the contract-as-product model is to be adopted, then the law must provide clarity as to what terms will be integral to the product and what terms will not. This applies especially to tangible products as it seems nonsensical, for example, to purport that a choice of forum clause is integral to the product.

Exclusion Clauses and Rights Deletion

As it has been previously noted, standard form contracts are devised intentionally to benefit the business that uses it. With a superior bargaining position combined, this self-interest comes at the expense of denying consumers of particular rights.

Exclusion clauses are just one of many types of term that are incorporated into standard form contracts. Although these are perfectly legitimate, they have come under close judicial and legislative scrutiny. Exclusion clauses are a useful tool for businesses to exclude their liability or limit it; allocating the liability upon the consumer. Prior to protectionist legislation, the courts had limited ability in protecting the consumer against unfair terms and exclusion clauses. However, they have succeeded in adopting an approach of a restrictive nature against their interpretation.

The courts use the *contra preferentum* rule which has the effect of interpreting any ambiguity in a term strictly against the party seeking to rely on it (i.e. the business)[67]. Although this rule has applied stringently to exclusion clauses, it is nevertheless applicable to any ambiguous term in a contract[68]. This rule has been effectively applied in the case of *Andrew Bros Ltd v Singer Cars*[69]. In this case, Andrew Bros contracted with Singer

---

[67] Ewan McKendrick, *Contract Law* (9th edn, Palgrave Macmillan 2011) p.190.
[68] Ibid.
[69] [1934] 1 KB 17

Cards for the purchase of "new Singer cars". The contract contained a term which excluded "all conditions, warranties and liabilities implied by statute, common law or otherwise". One of the cars that had been delivered was not new and had been previously used on the roads. Andrew Bros sought to reject the car but Singer Cars claimed that their exclusion clause was effective to prevent to prevent Andrew Bros from doing so. The courts held the standard form clause was ineffective because it did not cover the loss in question and interpreted it strictly against the party seeking to rely on it. Although this case involves two businesses as opposed to a business-consumer relationship, the principle would be applied in the same manner.

The doctrine of notice is also an important tool for the courts to use in protecting the consumer against an aversion of their rights. This places considerable responsibility on part of the business to ensure that their terms are given sufficient notice if they wish to rely on them. Although we have looked at the significance of a signature in incorporating standard terms into a contract, notice is also an important method. In *Interfoto Picture Library v Stiletto Visual Programmes Ltd*[70] the court held that a holding fee clause was not incorporated into the contract because insufficient notice had been given to the defendant of its terms. It held that a party who seeks to incorporate into a contract a term which

---

[70] [1989] QB 433.

is particularly onerous or unusual must prove that term has been reasonably and fairly drawn to the attention of the other party[71]. This resonates in the judgment of Denning LJ in *Spurling v Bradshaw*[72] in which he made reference to "big red hands" – some clauses would need to have a "large red hand pointing to it on the face of the document" before the notice would be regarded as sufficient. Although it is an attempt by the courts to improve the position of the consumer, it still falls short of ensuring any genuine understanding of the terms. It is often the case that clauses are held to be part of the agreement even though the business knows full well they have neither been read nor understood.

---

[71] Ibid.

[72] [1956] EWCA Civ 3

In terms of legislative protection, the first significant piece was provided to consumers in the late 70's with the Unfair Contract Terms Act[73]. It must be noted that this legislation only applies to exclusion and limitation clauses. It could be argued that this was because Parliament recognised most unfair terms took the form of exclusion clauses. This is a powerful piece of legislation and grants the courts significant powers in rendering terms invalid. For instance, UCTA restricts clauses that exclude liability for death or personality injury caused by negligence[74]. However, when it comes to other loss or damage (proprietary etc), liability cannot be excluded unless the term satisfies a test of

---

[73] Unfair Contract Terms Act 1977

[74] UCTA 1977, s2(1)

"reasonableness"[75]. UCTA also provides consumer protection when they are dealing "on the other's written standard terms of business"[76], specifically meaning standard form contracts. The protection this section aims to provide is when the exclusion clause claims entitlement to render a contractual performance substantially different from what was reasonably expected of him[77] or to render no performance at all[78]. This is a significant regulation upon standard form contracts as it is a seemingly obvious protection. I contend that this legislative provision is Parliament's recognition that businesses can attempt to incorporate such clauses into a contract because they acknowledge

---

[75] UCTA 1977, s2(2).
[76] UCTA 1977, s3(1)
[77] UCTA 1977 s3(2)
[78] Ibid.

consumers have the propensity to sign contracts without giving them due care and consideration. This gives room for severe exploitation on part of the business. It is legislative acknowledgement that consumers cannot be expected to read standard form contracts in their contemporary convoluted state.

Europe has also added to the consumer protectionist dimension. The Unfair Terms in Consumer Contract Regulations[79] affords a wider scope of protection to consumers than that of UCTA. The regulations state that an unfair term creates a "serious imbalance in the parties' rights and obligations under the contract to the

---

[79] UTCCR 1999.

detriment of the consumer[80]. Unlike UCTA, UTCCR applies to all unfair terms and has been argued to give consumers a much broader protection from unfair terms in standard form contracts[81]. It must be noted that the UTCCR gives more focus to standard form contracts than UCTA does, as it only applies to contracts that are not individually negotiated[82]. The regulations describe a non-individually negotiated term as "...drafted in advance and the consumer has therefore not been able to influence the substance of the term"[83]. In the finding of an

---

[80] UTCCR 1999, s5(1).

[81] Ewan McKendrick, *Contract Law: Text, Cases, and Matierlas* (3rd edn, OUP 2008), p.8 .

[82] UTCCR 1999, s5(1).

[83] UTCCR 1999 s5(2).

unfair term, the regulations hold it not to be binding on the consumer[84].

In assessment of the legislation, it can be argued that the Courts and Parliament acknowledge the problems that arise in standard form contracts between businesses and consumers. However, the protections afforded to the consumer only come into action when an innocent party has been wronged. It assumes that the standard form contracts will purport to contain these clauses and will deal with them as and when a dispute arises. If a consumer were to read their contract and found a clause that stipulated "we exclude all liability for death or personal injury on our

---

[84] UTCCR 1999 s8(1).

premises", the claimant would not be able to complain to the court as the court would find itself unable to act until such death or personal injury occurred. Although this clause would be invalidated without question, the courts' power to invalidate a term is relatively weak. The law should not wait for the wrong to happen and should be able to act in a deterring/preventive fashion. Although similarities lie within the field of criminal law (in that the law only comes into effect when there's a crime), criminal law has penal consequences for attempted criminal acts. Criminal attempts[85] are arguably an effective measure at deterring people endeavouring to commit criminal activity. Perhaps the same level

---

[85] See Criminal Attempts Act 1981.

of deterrence could be translated into the contract arena and hold businesses accountable for attempting to adopt such exploitative practices.

Furthermore, the legislation does nothing to encourage consumers to read the terms nor does it do anything to ensure a genuine understanding of the terms. I submit that this is because Parliament does not expect any utility to come from it – even if the consumer reads the terms, it is unlikely they would understand its substance and impact.

The above discussion relates to the issues in standard form contracts and the application of legislation in paper form. Gomulkiewicz argues that although the electronic standard form contract is thriving, paper form still dominates[86]. As it is a new dynamic to the arena, standard terms used by companies selling electronic goods and services may remain relatively untested in the courts[87]. It is nevertheless problematic for consumers as e-commerce is but another forum in which businesses can exploit them. As discussed earlier, businesses can easily manipulate the presentation of their terms on websites, making it even less likely for consumers to read them. This allows, according to Radin, a rights deletion[88] schemes to exist with

---

[86] Robert W. Gomulkiewicz 'The License is the Product: Comments on the Promise of Article 2B for Software and Information Licensing' [1998] Berkley Technology Law Journal 891.

[87] Ibid at p.45.

[88] Margaret J. Radin, 'Boilerplate: The Fine Print, Vanishing Rights, and The Rule of Law' (Princeton University Press, 2013) .

relative ease. It can be argued that the digital age is but a playground for businesses to induce customers into quick contracting whilst depriving the consumer of particular rights, in a manner which exploits their unmindfulness. Although online boilerplate is relatively new, it will be interesting to see how the courts approaches disputes. It may be the case that like in the paper world, the courts show a relative degree of deference to the expertise of businesses. This would be unfortunate as online boilerplate gives greater justification for a higher degree of judicial oversight.

Radin: Political and Normative Degradation

So far we have looked at the practical implications for the consumer. However, it is prudent to look at the broader implications of standard form contracting for our political system. Although the literature discusses these theoretical implications in relation to paper standard form, I see no good reason to ascribe the same implications to e-commerce. It could even be argued that electronic contracting has opened doors to further degradation, coming without the scrutiny it so deserves.

Normative degradation is a term used by Margaret Radin in her seminal work[89] and refers

---

[89] Margaret J. Radin, 'Boilerplate: The Fine Print, Vanishing Rights, and The Rule of Law' (Princeton University Press, 2013) p.19

to "...the fact that our own system is committed to the moral premise that justifies our legal structure of contract enforcement, that premise being that people who enter contracts are voluntarily giving up something in exchange for something they value more"[90]. What Radin means by this is that legal systems enforce contracts because they value freedom of contract based on voluntary consent. Radin talks of a degradation coming from the notion that consumers do not read the terms when it comes to boilerplate contracts. Standard form contracts include clauses which can exclude liability on part of the business, or even determine how disputes are to be resolved (often out of court). Radin talks

---

[90] Ibid at p.15.

about a "deletion of rights" thematically throughout her work and it refers to the idea that consumers agree to unseen boilerplates; which deny them of particular rights. I agree with Radin when it comes to her argument concerning boilerplate clauses make for a deletion of rights. The normative degradation comes in as boilerplates "allow businesses to take away the right of others without their consent"[91]. As discussed continuously, the reality is that consumers are seldom informed when it comes to their rights (or lack of) in standard form. This essentially degrades the foundational ide that people contract on a voluntary basis. Radin also contends that boilerplate allows for a "political

---

[91] Ibid.

degradation", which stems from its normative counterpart[92]. She argues:

"Mass market systems of form contracts that restructure the rights of users of products and services operate to undermine or cancel the rights of users granted by legislatures"[93].

Radin argues that mass market boilerplates displace legal regimes enacted by states when it "withdraws a number of important recipients' rights"[94]. It has been suggested that the "private ordering"[95] creates a tension with the rules

---

[92] Ibid at p.16.

[93] Ibid.

[94] Ibid at p.33

[95] Private ordering has been described as distinct and stable rules or exchange between individuals, subject to their own individual will and not that of the state.

enacted by the state, allowing firms to devise their own legal universe[96]. This ultimately undermines the political order and rights granted to individuals. Therefore, it can be argued that within the realms of private contractual negotiations, contract law has developed in a way that allows firms to utilise mass market contracts that encompasses their own legal universe; subjecting recipients to a loss of their rights afforded to them by the polity. This raises democratic degradation arguments as the state is a democratic body, elected by the recipients of these draconian contracts. The state grants these protectionist rights in the interests of the electorate. To allow firms to deny individuals of

---

[96] Margaret J. Radin, 'Boilerplate: The Fine Print, Vanishing Rights, and The Rule of Law' (Princeton University Press, 2013) p.33.

these conferred rights is to undermine the State's authority. Access to courts has been a long-standing cornerstone of democracy afforded to the citizenry, which is easily deniable by the use of an arbitration clause. It is interesting to note that arbitration clauses are given much negative perception despite its use being a response to the inefficiencies inherent within the court system. Arbitration is considered a faster, simpler, and cheaper method of dispute resolution in contrast to litigation. However, arbitration is a cause for concern as it is questionable as to whether an arbitration tribunal enjoys the same level of independence and freedom from external pressures that the judiciary do.

Modularity

Although the digital age has created many causes for concern, it has also facilitated a practice which is unique to it. Modularity has architectural derivations, referring to the practice of building a whole by using things that already exist; analogous to construction with building blocks[97]. In the standardisation of boilerplate and its evolution to e-commerce, modularity has grown in legal significance. Radin describes legal modularity as "the practice of creating a legal document by selecting and cobbling together terms from a source compendium or from different sources"[98]. Boilerplate has modularity

---

[97] Margaret J. Radin, 'Boilerplate Today: The Rise of Modularity and Waning of Consent' [2006] Michigan Law Review 1223.

[98] Ibid at p.1224.

potential due to its standardised nature: the standard terms can be likened to the building block in the creation of a contract. This means that standard form contracts can be customised by selecting particular uniform terms. It has been argued that this selecting of particular terms has been largely facilitated by digitisation[99]. This is because computing has allowed for documents to be varied; copying and pasting different clauses with ease and being able to redistribute. Radin notes three implications to modularity caused by digitisation. First, standardised clauses can be routinely organised even for small transactions[100]. Second, combining particular terms can be routinely copied and utilised by other businesses.

---

[99] Ibid.
[100] Ibid.

This has been described as "modularity free-riding"[101]. Third, digitisation facilitates an automation in contracting[102].

In the first implication, modularity allows for even the smallest of transaction to be customised, tailoring them to the needs of the consumer. This is ever prevalent on shopping websites; consumers can select their preferred method of delivery, each option varying in cost and time. Although this variation is slight, it opens doors to wider customisation. Customers could find themselves having to pay extra to have their contract governed by a legal system of their

---

[101] Ibid.
[102] Ibid.

choosing[103] or opting for an out-of-court resolution of dispute.. Although this reduces the take-it-or-leave it fashion and one-sidedness of boilerplate contracts, modularity is still problematic for the consumer. Even if the consumer is mindful enough to customise the contract, it is very likely they will only be concerned with the "on the face of it" description. The terms may have simplistic descriptions but could be underpinned by a degree of complexity. Modularity and customisation do nothing for the consumer's understanding of the terms and their implications; it just offers choice. One may opt to have their contract governed by the law of their country, but that does nothing to inform them of

---

[103] This is also known as a choice of forum clause.

what it actually entails. When it comes to the selection of particular terms, the ability to compare them and determine which will be most beneficial will only be available to the most diligent consumer. If a business offers varying contract terms, it would be prudent to mitigate the risk with price. Therefore it will be in their interest to charge more for terms which allocate more risk to them, or is the least onerous on the consumer. This means that the most appealing contracts will only be available to the wealthiest consumers.

The second implication refers to the possibility of widespread standardisation. Digitised clauses can be copied instantly and the internet allows for worldwide availability[104]. This will allow for firms to adopt the customised terms and will see a trend in using successful clauses. As previously argued, a lot of online boilerplate remains largely untested, but digitisation will allow for rapid free-riding once testing has begun[105].

In relation to the third implication, modularity in digitised contracts facilitates automatic agreements being formed[106]. The automation would depend on routine contracting based upon an ongoing relationship between A and B. Radin argues that these automated contracts would be

---

[104] Margaret J. Radin, 'Boilerplate Today: The Rise of Modularity and Waning of Consent' [2006] Michigan Law Review 5 1223. p.1226.

[105] For more discussion on business' understanding of the effect of clauses, see Michelle Boardman, 'Contra Preferentum: The Allure of Ambiguous Boilerplate' [2006] Michigan Law Review 1114.

[106] Margaret J. Radin, 'Boilerplate Today: The Rise of Modularity and Waning of Consent' [2006] Michigan Law Review 5 1223. p.1226.

facilitated by computers programme with a specific input, such as a specific search of terms[107]. Again, this would provide time and cost benefits as it would only require an initial program, then variations according to need. It is pertinent to note that this would not be suitable for all types of contract, just those of a routine nature, such as agreements between traders and suppliers. As this book focuses primarily on consumer contracts, it is difficult to see how automation would be beneficial to them, for reasons stated above.

In summary, boilerplates in the digital arena has allowed for modularity to grow in significance. In

---

[107] Ibid.

uniformity of terms, the internet has become a tool which enables consumers to combine particular terms to suit their choosing. Although Radin cast this in a positive light, the literature suggests further implications. Combining particular terms is only beneficial to the consumer that appreciates their implications, and can compare them to the alternatives and afford them. As I have argued previously, it makes economic sense for businesses to offer the varying terms in accordance with a suitable price. The more risk it allocates on the business, the more expensive for the consumer it will be. Therefore consumers may be saddled with less favourable terms because of cost implications. Modularity in the digital age also facilitates the rapid free-riding of successful terms which have been rested in courts. Although this has not been the case yet, it is a reasonable prediction. When this becomes the case, it also means that businesses will adopt the more expensive terms which are least beneficial to them, thus driving up the price of appealing contracts. Therefore, thee will not only be a free-riding of successful terms, but of the cost attached to them too.

Regulatory Solutions

As discussed earlier, reforms to the standard and relationship of consent has been given more attention than to the reform of standard form contracting itself. This section will consider reforms to the legal infrastructure and how standard form contracts can return back to a better standard of consent. The thematic issue throughout this book has always been the perpetual unmindfulness of the consumer; the lack of expectation on the consumer to read the contract and the reality of them not doing so. The regulatory reforms which are to be discussed ameliorate these issues both in the paper and digital worlds. One important reform that can be afforded to the standard form contracting arena is to increase the level of judicial oversight granted to the treatment boilerplate clauses. In its most radical form, this would be to abolish or invalidate standard form contracts, which purport to alter or deprive the consumer of their rights. This would take issue with the degradation of consent which has occurred, rendering" blanket assent" inapplicable. This reform will not be given much contemplation as it is a mere extremity, only to be a sort of ideal which would have no place in today's contracting. To implement a reform which invalidates exclusory clauses would see a large decline in the use of standard form contracting. Businesses would have no control in allocating risks, and thus prices for products would escalate exponentially. Businesses may also stray away from engaging in particular transactions which require a relative degree of risk allocation, such as ownership of car parks.

Effective reforms would focus on incentivising consumers to read the terms of their contract, in an attempt to bring about a "meeting of minds" to the contractual table. In the electronic arena, Hillman proposes some solutions which aim to make the consumer mindful of their position prior to the agreement[108]. He argues that a mandatory disclosure of e-boilerplates could assist in bringing the terms to the attention to the consumer[109]. This would require "...a business to maintain an internet presence and to post its

---

[108] Robert A. Hillman 'Online Boilerplate: Would Mandatory Website Disclosure of E-Standard Terms Backfire?' [2006] Cornell Law Faculty Publications 542

[109] Ibid.

terms prior to any particular transaction, so that a consumer could read and compare terms without making a purchase at all"[110]. A business could display their terms on their homepage, which is often a consumer's primary visit. If not displayed on the homepage, a clearly identified hyperlink could be placed. As mentioned earlier, businesses have used the internet as a tool to cleverly manipulate the presentation of their terms. Businesses alter the way in which terms are presented, through the use of different displays, graphics, and font. This reform goes to the heart of this manipulation and calls for a presentation of terms in an acceptable manner. Although Hillman uncovers the potential benefits

---

[110] Ibid at p.838.

of this mandatory disclosure, he is cautious of the backfire it could have in making suspect terms more likely enforceable[111].

For Hillman, this reform would create an increase in the number of consumers who read the terms. He persuasively argues that, even if the disclosure did not increase the number of consumers reading the terms, it might nevertheless incentivise businesses to write fairer terms[112]. I agree with him in that the opportunity of consumers being more mindful would loom over the heads of many businesses, fearing the repercussions of consumers becoming aware of the unfavourable terms. My issue with this is that

---

[111] Ibid.

[112] Ibid at p.839.

although there will be improvement to the display of terms, this does not necessarily make them easier to read. Display does nothing to improve the clarity or length of clauses; it just makes it easier to find the convolution. This reform would however see a return to the reasonable expectation to read the terms and to be thus bound by what has been signed.

Hillman also notes that consumers who have a better opportunity to read and compare terms would reinforce Llewellyn's "blanket assent" rhetoric to reasonable standard terms. This point does have a degree of accuracy as consumers would find it hard to argue they have provided something short of consent.

In short, a mandatory website disclosure of terms would provide consumers with a greater opportunity to read the terms, allowing them to become more knowledgeable of their position. It could be argued that this is bringing Lord Denning's "big red hands" approach to the digital arena[113] and that consumers could find less of a complaint in suggesting that what they have provided is something short of true consent. Even if it does not improve the rate of consumers reading the terms, the potential would be enough arguably to incentivise businesses to strive towards fair practice. However, as I have argued, this is merely a practical solution and does nothing to improve the substance of the terms. It

---

[113] For discussion of Lord Denning's "big red hands", see Spurling v Bradshaw [1956] EWCA Civ 3.

is widely accepted that boilerplate contracts are convoluted and contain legal jargon. A mandatory disclosure of these terms only makes it easier to find them and does nothing to aid consumers' understanding of them.

The above reform highlights an interesting argument in that it could incentivise businesses to adopt a fairer practice when it comes to devising boilerplate clauses. This incentive comes from the idea that consumers have a greater opportunity to review the clauses, being better able to uncover unfair terms. It is pertinent to note that not only would businesses worry about consumers uncovering such terms, but would worry about a watch-dog exposure of such terms[114]. This leads to another reform in order to improve the problems which arise in standard form contracting. A third party agency could be established to monitor and review standard form contracts which are used by firms in business-consumer transactions. It is interesting to note that this reform can be both market and regulatory (depending on its control) and can apply to both the paper and virtual arena. Parliament could establish an independent third party organisation whose tasks is to review standard form contracts and to continuously monitor them.

---

[114] Robert A. Hillman, 'Online Boilerplate: Would Mandatory Website Disclosure of E-Standard Terms Backfire?' [2006] Cornell Law Faculty Publications 542 p.846.

This third party organisation could be granted a wide range of powers ranging from reviewing contracts, to amending them. To give the substantive reform which was missing from the mandatory disclosure requirement, this organisation could be given the task of simplifying terms in a manner which consumers would understand. This organisation would be acting in a watch-dog fashion but be granted powers by the State. It could even go as far as publishing the names of businesses which have adopted unsavoury terms. This would create an indefinite incentive for businesses to transact fairly with consumers in fear of having their reputation tarnished. This agency could even develop a set of "model" terms which strike an effective balance between business interests and the rights of the consumer.

For the sake of description, this agency could be called the "Standard Form Consumer Contracts Authority" (SFCCA). In terms of structure, it could be staffed by lawyers who could be skilled in understanding standardised clauses and could relay them into terms that consumers would appreciate. Being granted powers by Parliament, it could be accountable to the Department of Business Innovation and Skills; this department currently oversees consumer protection and therefore this agency would fall within its remit.

In light of online contracting, this agency could provide a benefit unique to it. As previously mentioned, online contracts have found themselves updatable with relative ease, also bearing the same level of unmindfulness found in the initial agreement. Software updates often come with TOS and COU updates in tandem. As such, it could be the responsibility of this agency to continuously monitor the updates and publish the implications (if any).

In relation to the presentation of terms on websites, consumers could have more confidence in dealing with businesses online that have received a stamp of approval from the hypothetical "SFCCA". As e-commerce is big on graphics and imagery on websites, much can be said about the appeal of having a token which says "SFCCA approved". This imagery is so simplistic yet can instil a great deal of confidence in consumers when dealing with businesses.

In summation, standard form contracts are of such popular use in business-consumer transactions that it could justify the implementation of an independent third party authority, with the responsibility of overseeing standard form contracts devised by firms and to continuously monitor online agreements. To give it hypothetical description, it has been referred to as the "Standard Form Consumer Contracts Authority". The SFCCA could be granted powers by the State to review and monitor standard form contracts which have the sole purpose of being used for business-consumer transactions. It could make terms more user friendly in our search for understandable boilerplate. It would perform a watch-dog role and comes with legislative teeth. To appeal to the imagery and display of e-commerce, the use of an SFCCA stamp of approval could provide a great deal of confidence to consumers and the market.

At present, the Financial Conduct Authority, and the Competition & Markets Authority are two bodies which are responsible for the regulation of firms and protection of consumer interests. The FCA is a body which is funded by the firms that it regulates, being accountable to The Treasury[115]. It has supervisory powers and grants authorisation to businesses to perform certain

---

[115] http://www.fca.org.uk/about accessed 11th April 2016

activities. In relation to boilerplate, the FCA has the power to challenge unfair terms in standard form contracts. However, the FCA cannot involve itself in individual disputes consumers may have with firms[116]. The Competition & Markets Authority is a non-ministerial department and as the name suggests, regulates affairs related to business competition. It oversees business activity and monitors anti-trust offences[117]. Although these agencies are accountable to Parliament and are responsible for overseeing consumer protection, standard form contracts only form a minor part of their oversight. In relation to the FCA, they cannot become involved

---

[116] http://www.fca.org.uk/forms/being-regulated/unfair-contracts/our-powers accessed 11th April 2016.

[117] http://www.gov.uk/government/organisations/competition-and-markets-authority/about#responsibilities accessed 11th April 2016.

with individual cases and thus retain and outsider approach towards consumer protection in standard form contracts. The proposed SFCCA could fill this gap and become directly involved in consumer cases, thus performing a regulatory and representative role.

One actual reform that has recently come into legislative force is the Consumer Rights Act 2015. The CRA 2015 is a consolidating piece of legislation which came into force in October 2015. This is the first piece of legislation to bring clear consumer protection when purchasing digital content[118]. The CRA applies the same implied terms[119] that are provided in tangible

---

[118] Consumer Rights Act 2015, ch3.
[119] Consumer Rights Act 2015, s34-s40.

goods and services contracts[120]. It is also

interesting to note that the CRA makes provision

for contracts where a trader supplies digital

content to a consumer with the right to modify

the digital content[121]. The CRA allows for such

modification to the extent that it seeks to

improve the features, or adds features to the

digital content. The modification is subject to it

continuing to match the description of the original

content provided by the trader[122] and conforms to

the information provided by the trader[123]. This

provision links directly to the issue discussed

earlier in the book with regards to updating

---

[120] Implied terms offered by the Sales of Goods Act 1979 and the Supply of Goods and Services Act 1981.

[121] Consumer Rights Act 2015, s40.

[122] Consumer Rights Act, s40(2)(a)

[123] Consumer Rights Act 2015, s40(2)(b)

software and terms. There is now clear legislation purporting to prevent businesses from updating or altering their contracts and products, to the extent it no longer reflects the initial agreement.

In relation to unfair terms, the CRA requires written terms or consumer notices to be transparent[124]. The Act regards transparency as "...if it is expressed in plain and intelligible language and is legible"[125]. It can be argued that this provision is bringing common law controls into legislative force. The powers of the courts remain the same as they were granted by UCTA; being able to render an unfair term invalid. Therefore, the law has done nothing for the

---

[124] Consumer Rights Act 2015, s68(1).
[125] Consumer Rights Act 2015, s69(2).

efficacy of the courts' powers, with invalidation being a relatively weak recourse. Thus, the proposed SFCCA still stands to be strong proposal despite this new legislation.

Market Solutions

The above discussion relates to improving standard form in a regulatory manner, by way of judicial and legislative controls. However, there is a body of literature which aims to improve the position of standard form contracting outside of the legal scope. Some academics content that improvement to business-consumer standard form transactions should come from market forces.

Radin highlights some interesting private solutions which do not necessarily focus on bringing the term to the attention of the consumer in the literal sense[126]. Radin suggests

---

[126] Margaret J. Radin, 'Boilerplate: The Fine Print, Vanishing Rights, and the Rule of Law' (Princeton University Press, 2013) ch10.

that a rating agency could be organised for the purpose of reviewing and rating the terms offered by companies. This solution does not attempt to amend or alter the terms offered, but categorises and casts them in a light which the consumer can use in their decision-making process. I said it does not bring the terms to the attention of the consumer in the literal sense because this solution does not aim to assist the consumer in their understanding of the term. Rather, it places the terms in binary categories of "appealing" and "unappealing", in a broad fashion. This label differs slightly from that offered by the SFCCA as the approval by the SFCCA could come having amended a firm's terms. The SFCCA would have democratic legitimacy, a quality that cannot be afforded to rating agencies outside of the regulatory scope. This does have practical benefits for the consumer as it means they can make a more relatively informed decision when it comes to transacting with particular businesses; without the laborious task of reading the contract. This empowers customers to understand the positives and detriments of the contract and knowing what form they take, without actually having to read the entire document. This appeases Llewellyn's "blanket assent" theory in that a consumer will know if a contract contains a term which is adverse to their position and thus cannot argue they have provided something short of consent. This links well to the market solution of having a comparison-type website.

As already discussed, it is unlikely that consumers will be interested in anything other than the descriptive terms such as price and quality, and thus shop in a comparative nature. Although this raises questions regarding the "seal of approval" offered by the rating agency and the SFCA, the SFCCA's label would have greater force and trust behind it; as it comes from a legislative authority. Rating agencies could give their rating (their own stamp of approval) based on the terms in front of them; without having any capacity to alter them. The SFCCA could work with firms to ensure their terms are fair and reasonable, amending them if they fall short. Therefore the stamp of approval offered by the SFCCA could represent cooperation between the agency and the business.

In devising a website which creates a comparison for contractual terms other than the immediately-descriptive, this will allow for consumers to shop in a comparative nature but with greater terms in mind. My issue with these solutions is that it may exacerbate consumer complacency and nonchalance in not reading the terms. Entering contracts will no longer be down to a consumer's own bounded rationality and will be unduly influenced by a third party. The funding of the agency is also a question which should be paid some regard. Perhaps the rating agency could be funded by the firms it rates, akin to the funding of the FCA by the firms it regulates. The notion of having a comparison and rating of terms is precariously descriptive and furthers the disinterest consumers have with their legal position. It may also be problematic to encapsulate a wide and diverse range of terms into a binary list which suggests the term is either "appealing" or "unappealing". This isolates the term from a contract and gives it a description which may be significantly different from it being taken in the context of the contract itself. Description is also subjective and thus heavy reliance is placed upon the accuracy given by the agency purporting it.

Conclusion

To conclude this book, we have looked at the historical position of "agreement" within the scope of contract law. Once being a concept requiring a subjective "meeting of minds", judicial developments have saw a shift towards an objectivity of contract. As such, objectivity demanded a duty to read the terms of a contract and acknowledgement of this duty took the form of signature. In upholding certainty, the courts stipulated that a signature binds a person to a contract irrespective of reading the terms. This principle became problematic when standard form contracts evolved, which we have seen revolutionise the agreement paradigm between businesses and consumers. We have come to understand standard form contracts as a one-sided agreement, devised by a firm with the intention of repeated use in transacting. These forms are devised intentionally to serve a firm's best interests, which often come at the expense of the rights of the consumer. Justifications of standard form have also been consider. These justifications link directly to the economic benefits and necessity that they provide.

In developing our understanding of boilerplate contracts in the digital age, we analysed similarities and differences with its paper counterpart, uncovering particular advantages to the e-consumer. There is an absence of social pressure in the virtual arena, meaning a customer will not feel pressured into agreement by an agent of the company, who may present a pushed-for-time atmosphere. It has been argued that a consumer who transacts online can do so in their own privacy, with more time to acquaint themselves with the terms of the contract. However, I have argued that this opportunity to read has not been fully utilised and consumers still find themselves relatively unaware of the terms. The lack of a live agent in the online forum is problematic as there is no one to aid the consumer in understanding the terms.

We have seen divided opinion related to the significance of a "click" and whether it holds the same legal significance to that of a signature on a paper contract. It can be said that however that there is a consensus in believing clicking "I agree" comes with the same level of complacency and underestimation as is with signing a contract. It is no secret that standard form contracts are lengthy and imbibed with legalese. A consumer cannot be reasonably expected to read these contracts and the virtual arena further supports this contestation. Businesses can use the internet as a manipulative tool to present the terms in a deceptive fashion, if at all.

Current judicial and legislative measures have been scrutinised and that this shift to a "consumer protection" culture suggests an acknowledgement by Parliament that the law on standard form contract at present is unsatisfactory and this is underpinned by the correct assumption that consumers cannot be expected to read them. This is also acknowledgement of the fact that businesses recognise consumers do not read their contract and attempt to use this as a means of implementing exploitative and onerous terms. In assessing the legislation, I have argued that the current measures only have impact when a dispute arises and does nothing to aid the consumer prior to the agreement. I have called for a regime which assists the consumer in their pre-contractual position: techniques which bring the terms to the attention of the consumer in a simplified and understandable fashion.

Theoretical implications offered by Margaret Radin have also been considered in great depth, uncovering how boilerplate has contributed to the normative degradation of our understanding of freedom to contract. Radin has also explored the idea of political degradation in that the boilerplate arena has allowed firms to devise their own legal universes, in which rights granted to consumers by the State have no place and are thus deleted in contract.

In coming to understand the contemporary nature of digital boilerplate, I have discussed the concept of modularity and how the electronic arena has allowed for a degree of customisation with particular terms; allowing standard form contracts to become tailored to consumers. I have uncovered issues in that customising the most consumer-beneficial contract will only be available to consumers that can afford them. This means that cost-conscious consumers will be saddled with the contract that greater benefits the business.

This book has also looked at academic debate which attempts to reconceptualise our traditional understanding off consent and its relationship with contract. As standard form contracting has led to a reduction in the standard of consent require to formulate a binding agreement, scholars have devised a relationship between consent and contract which pertains to hold the terms to be integral to the product of the contract, and not as a distinct bargain. I have unveiled arguments which suggest that this is problematic as contracts in the digital age have unlimited scope for continuous development. Shrinkwrap and browsewrap agreements often come with an updated TOS/COU. If we were to adhere to this contract-as-product model, it would allow for the nature of the product to be justifiably modified.

In analysing the conventional issues that consumers face with standard form contracts, assessing the implications in a digital context has allowed us to uncover further implications, which in turn further supports the need for intervention. I submit that the current oversight of standard form contracts is insufficient and the digital age warrants the need for further intervention. Legislative reforms have been considered, with one being cautious of a mandatory online disclosure regime. Instead, I advocate the implementation of an independent third party agency which is accountable to the State. It will be an independent organisation with statutory powers to review and modify standard form contracts used by businesses to transact with consumers. This comes in tandem with a statutory duty upon businesses to submit their contracts for review. I have also suggested that in ameliorating the issues with online contracts being continuous, the SFCCA will be responsible for overseeing any updates to firm TOS/COUs and publish any implications which consumers may face as a result. I have noted a benefit which may be conferred on businesses in their compliance, in using a "stamp of approval" on their website. This will appeal to consumers as it instils confidence in their transactions.

Market reforms have also been considered which take the form of description. Rating agencies and comparison forums provide consumers with a simplified knowledge of the terms and categorises them into either "appealing" or "unappealing". I have taken issue with this and contend that market pressures are not sufficient to improve the position of the consumer. I submit that any reform to the standard form environment must come from the State as I am sceptical to any improvement coming without legal teeth. There is much to be done in bringing the consumer into a more mindful position, and this can be achieved by improving their pre-contractual position. Consumer autonomy and freedom to contract are two important principles which must be preserved. This preservation can come about by aiding them in their

understanding of the terms. The law should

attempt to place the consumer in the most

knowledgeable position possible, for their

contractual agreements to be based on decisions

which are underpinned by an appreciation of the

terms; both beneficial and detrimental to them.

Bibliography

Journals

- Barnett R, 'Consenting to Form Contracts' (2002) 71 Fordham Law Review 627-645.

- Ben-Shahar O, 'The Myth of the Opportunity to Read' in Contract Law (July 18 2008), U of Chigago Law 7 Economics, Olin Working Paper no 415.

- Bix B, Contracts, The Ethics of Consent (Franklin G. Miller and Alan Wertheimer, eds., 2010)

- Boardman, M.E 'Contra Preferentum: The Allure of Ambiguous Boilerplate' (2006) 104 Michigan Law Review 1114-1118

- Eisenberg M.A, The Limits of Cognition and the Limits of Contract (1995) 47 Stanford Law Review 211

- Farnsworth A.E, ` Meaning in the Law of Contracts' (1967) 76 Yale Law Journal 939, 943-44

- Gomulkiewicz R, The License is the Product: Comments on the Promise of Article 2B for Software and Information Licensing (1998) 13 Berkley Tech 897

- Hillman R.A and Rachlinski JJ, Standard Form Contracting in the Electronic Age (2002) 77 New York University Law Review 2

- -- 'Online Boilerplate: Would Mandatory Website Disclosure of E-Standard Terms Backfire?' (20060 Cornell Law Faculty Publications 542.

- Johnston J.S, 'The Return of Bargain: An Economic Theory of how Standard Form Contracts Enable Cooperative Negotiation Between Businesses and Consumers' 104 Michigan Law Review 857 2005-2006.

- Kahan M, and Klausner M, 'Path Dependence in Corporate Contracting: Increasing Returns, Heard Behaviour, and Cognitive Biases' (1996) 74 Wash. U.L.Q 347.

- Kessler, F, 'Contracts of Adhesion – Some Thoughts About Freedom of Contract' (1943) Faculty Scholarship Series. Paper 2731.

- Llewellyn K, The Common Law Tradition: Deciding Appeals (1960).

- Macdonald E, 'Incorporation of Terms in Website Contracting – Clicking 'I agree'

(2011) 27 Journal of Contract Law, 198-222.

- Meyerson M.I, 'The Reunification of Contract Law: The Objective Theory of Consumer Form Contracts' (1993) 47 Miami Law Review 5.

- Prausnitz O, 'The Standardisation of Commercial Contracts in English and Continental Law' (1937) 52 Harvard Law Review 700.

- Preston C.B, 'Unwrapping Shrinkwraps, Clickwraps and Browsewraps: How the Law Went Wrong from Horse Traders to the

Law of the Horse' (2012) 26 Brigham

Young University Journal of Public Law 1.

- Radin M.J, 'Humans, Computers and

Binding Commitment' (2000) 75 Indiana

Law Journal 1125

- -- 'Boilerplate Today: The Rise of

Modularity and Waning of Consent' (2006)

104 Michigan Law Review 5 1223-1234.

- Rakoff T, 'Contracts of Adhesion, An Essay

in Reconstruction' (1983), 96 Harvard Law

Review 1173.

- Slawson, D.W, 'Standard Form Contracts

and Democratic Control of Lawmaking

Power' (1971) 84 Harvard Law Review 829.

Books

- Ben-Shahar O, Boilerplate: The Foundation of Market Contracts (1st edn, Cambridge University Press 2007).

- McKendrick E, Contract Law: Text, Cases and Materials (3rd edn, OUP 2008).

- -- Contract Law (9th edn, Palgrave Macmillan 2011)

- Radin M J, Boilerplate: The Fine Print, Vanishing Rights, and the Rule of Law (Princeton University Press, 2013).

- Wallace P, The Psychology of the Internet (1st edn, Cambridge University Press 2001)

Cases

- Andrew Bros Ltd v Singer Cars [1934] 1 KB 17

- Interfoto Picture Library v Stiletto Visual Programmes Ltd [1989] QB 433

- L'Estrange v Graucob [1934] 2 KB 934

- Smith v Hughes (1871) LR 6 QB 597 QBD

- Spurling v Bradshaw [1956] EWCA Civ 3

- Williams v America Online Inc (2001) WL
  135825

Legislation

- Unfair Contract Terms Act 1977

- Unfair Terms (Consumer Contracts)
  Regulations 1999

- Consumer Rights Act 2015

Websites

- http://windows.microsoft.com/en/gb/wido
  ws/update-microsoft-office#1TC=windows-
  7.

- http://www.fca.org.uk/about

- http://www.fca.org.uk/forms/being-regulated/unfair-contracts/our-powers

- http://www.gov.uk/government/organisations/competition-and-markets-authority/about#responsibilities